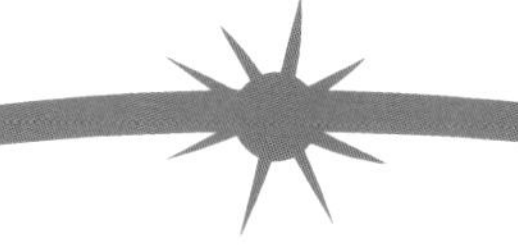

LOCURNA: STAR TRAVELLER

Blessings!
Wendy

Wendy Pierce, Ph.D.

Illustrated By: Natalie Fischer

To my mother who has always been, and continues to be, my inspiration. To my brother, Peter, for sharing his knowledge of science as we grew up and for sharing his ongoing love of nature. To my children, Cammie & Jake, whom I love dearly, and with love to Alysha & Kaydia, and for all future generations, that they may know of their unlimited potential and celebrate their connection to All That Is.

Balboa Press books may be ordered through booksellers or by contacting:

Balboa Press
A Division of Hay House
1663 Liberty Drive
Bloomington, IN 47403
www.balboapress.com
1 (877) 407-4847

Illustrated by: Natalie Fischer

ISBN: 978-1-5043-4047-2 (sc)
ISBN: 978-1-5043-4048-9 (e)

Library of Congress Control Number: 2016902521

Print information available on the last page.

Balboa Press rev. date: 4/8/2016
Printed in Canada

LOCURNA: STAR TRAVELLER

Wendy Pierce, Ph.D.

Illustrated By: Natalie Fischer

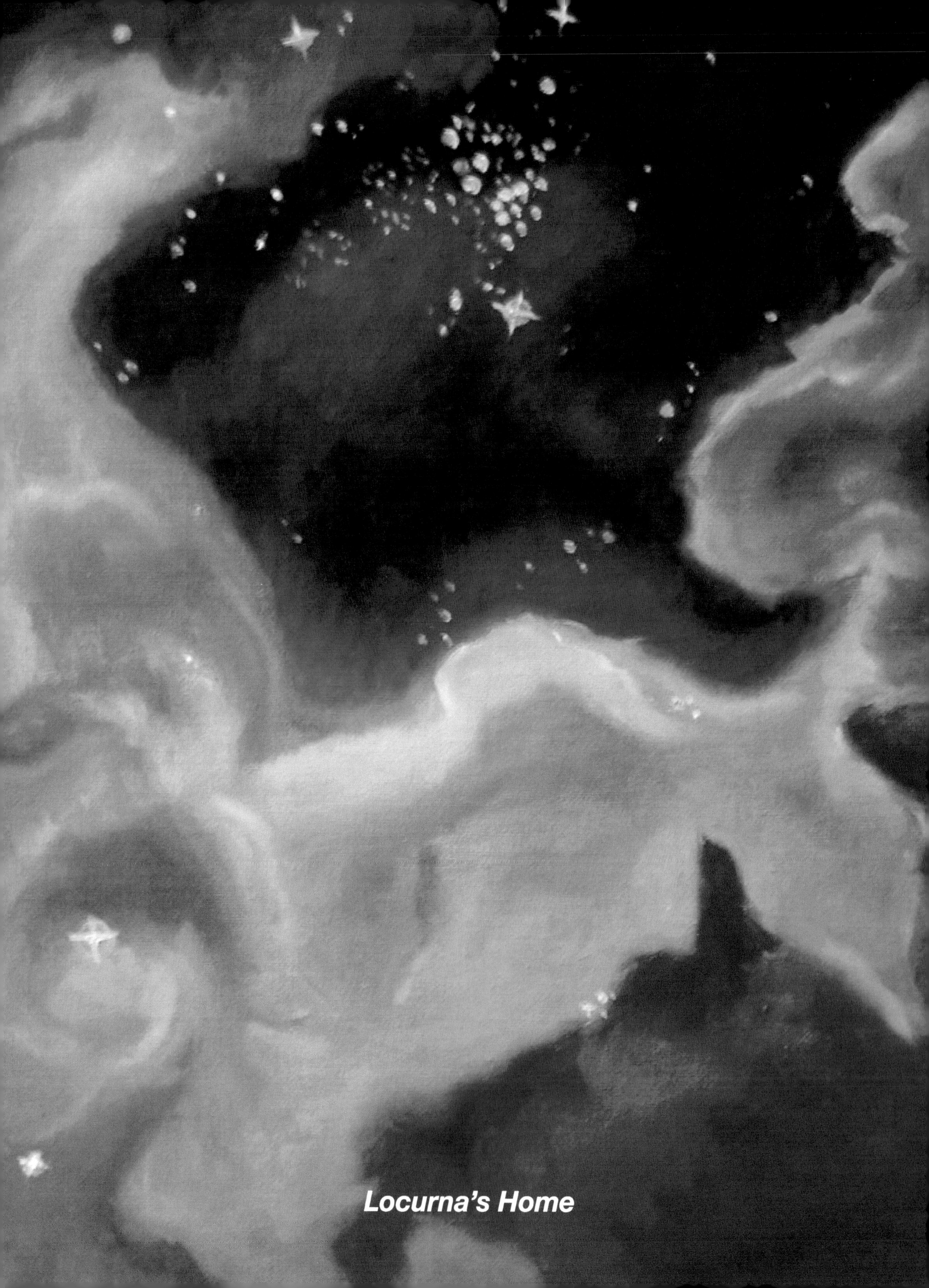

Locurna's Home

Hello, my name is Locurna. I am a Star Traveller and I come to you as a friend. I live very far away in Space which is way up in the sky farther than you can see. Other Star Travellers live here too and we know you and we all want to be your friends. Where we live is quite beautiful and we care about each other and enjoy our time together. Sometimes we move very fast amongst the stars and travel to wonderful places and sometimes we just like to float and twirl and move like you might do when you are in the water or perhaps on a swing. Did you know that the stars can be every colour? When you look at the stars they look white because they are so far away and you are just seeing their light. When we play amongst the stars it is like looking at the colours of a rainbow because the stars can be red, orange, yellow, green or blue and sometimes when all the stars are together they look like colourful clouds you can see through. When we move very fast the stars look like a long line of white streaks going by because all the colours blend together and look white. It is very quiet here because we are in space and because we are able to talk to each other just by THINKING about what we want to say! It is just like magic but we can do this because we are Spirits! Some people call Spirits Angels, but I like to be called Spirit because I am more of a ***feeling*** than a being. I am energy. All of the Star Travellers like being a part of ***All That Is***. This is sometimes called God but we like the spiritual name, ***All That Is***. This is because it includes every single thing in the world and out in space. But, the name is not the most important thing, it is the feeling of love for every single thing: for other people; for animals and plants; for the earth and the oceans; for all the stars and planets…***everything***. It is a love for each and every single thing and for ***All That Is***. This is a magical feeling and we would like to share it with you in this story and tell you our secrets because you are our friends and we want to help you understand.

The very first secret, and the most important one, is for you to love yourself. You are very special and you are an ***unlimited being***. This means that you can do anything you can think of because you are a part of ***All That Is***. The greatest gift you have been given is your imagination. You can do anything if you use your imagination. Just think of what you would like and then feel it with all your heart. Then you can ask the Star Travellers to help you to make it happen. This is a great idea and we call it "close your eyes and keep your heart wide open". This means you think about something and then start ***feeling*** it more than thinking of it so that you REALLY believe it. Then ask us for it and see yourself receiving or getting what you asked for and how happy it would make you feel and how thankful and grateful you would be. It might not happen right away but it will happen if you believe it with all your heart. This is how I came to talk to you in this story. I just thought about seeing you and being your friend and then I was here! Sometimes when people talk to the Star Travellers they can actually see them or hear them, just like having an imaginary friend, but this is a very special gift. If you are able to see or hear Spirit or feel them close by, it is nothing to be afraid of because it cannot hurt you, but not everyone is able to do this, so if you tell someone that you have this gift they may not understand. Sometimes just as you think of something, someone else says it or you just feel like they may say it. Sometimes it only happens once in a while but some people can do it all the time and it is okay if you can and it is okay if you can't because we are all different. You must try to understand when other people do not know what you are talking about and forgive them if they speak unkindly or if they don't understand. It is okay when we are all different and some of us can do special things and some of us can't. It is also okay for others to feel that they don't understand or don't want to know. Everyone is free to believe what they want and there is no right way or wrong way, there are just different ways to think or to do things.

The Star Travellers also like to play a game called ***"I imagine..."*** and you can play it too. If you would like to help someone who is sad or sick then you imagine them feeling better and send your thoughts of love to this person and ask the Star Travellers for their help. If you would like for everyone in the world to be friends with one another, then you can think really hard and send everyone love in your thoughts and ask the Star Travellers to help make it happen. Sometimes the Star Travellers just think of fun things to do like imagining flying in the sky like a bird and we see ourselves floating through the air and feeling happy. Sometimes we imagine what it would be like to swim in the ocean like a dolphin and to play and twirl in the water and have fun like they do. This is a great game because you can feel just like the bird or the dolphin and you can feel ***connected*** to them which is imagining how they feel. If you could be any animal what would it be? What would you be doing? Where would you be going? Anything that you can think about in your imagination can happen if you believe it and if you have trouble imagining just ask the Star Travellers to help you. Isn't that a wonderful secret? If you could make anything in the world happen what would you wish it to be? Just think of all the possibilities or things you could do! It might be something simple or something WONDERFUL! It works even better when you get together with your friends and you all imagine it happening. When all the Star Travellers want to do something wonderful we all get together and think very hard and we enjoy making things happen. When I wanted to come and see you, I travelled through the dark sky and saw all my friends, the other Star Travellers, and they lit up the sky for me with all the colours of the stars. As I was travelling to see you all the other Star Travellers were waving to me and some were keeping me company part of the way. It was very exciting! That is what it feels like when I travel amongst the stars and it is an awesome feeling. Would you like to travel amongst the stars? What do you think you might see? How do you think you would feel?

When the Star Travellers all get together we like to play a game called ***"How are you feeling?"*** Everyone is asked to say how they feel and why they feel happy or sad, angry or loving, mean or helpful, generous or selfish, tired or playful and that way everyone can try to understand why they feel the way they do. Do you know that every time you feel one way that there is also an opposite way of how to feel? This is normal and you can feel many different ways throughout the day. When you are sad or lonely or hurt it is nice to have someone cheer you up or give you a hug. When we do that for someone else it is called being compassionate or caring. Always treating others the same way you would like to be treated is doing your very best by trying to be kind. This makes them feel better and you can also feel better because you know you have done the right thing by helping someone else. When you are very happy isn't it nice to tell someone and see how happy they are for you? Also, when someone is telling you how happy they are then you can feel happy for them too! Just like my friends the Star Travellers who were so happy for me when they knew I was coming to talk to you. We all shared that same feeling and it was wonderful. It is great to have our families and our friends to help us this way and to share our feelings.

If you treat another person with respect this means that you try and talk nicely to them and you listen when they try to talk to you. People have different coloured skin and different thoughts or beliefs but you do not make fun of them for being different because deep down inside we all want to be treated kindly and loved for who we are. We all have a right to be respected for who we are and for the thoughts we have because all of us are important and special. Even if you are angry you must express it or say it so that people understand why, but you can still do this with kindness. You must take the time to explain why you feel angry and never say anything to hurt another person. It is okay to be angry but it is not okay to hurt someone else with your anger.

This is called being respectful and when you can use your words to tell someone about how you feel then you give them a chance to understand and help you to feel better. Wouldn't you like to be given the chance to feel better and to give someone else a chance to feel better too? Even if someone is angry with you or calls you names or tries to hit you, you tell them to stop and then instead of being angry with them you try and think about how they are feeling and why they are acting that way. If you can try to understand why they acted like they did then it is easier to forgive them. This is important for everyone to try and do.

So in our game we say, ***"How are you feeling?"*** and we wait for the other person to answer and sometimes they might be very sad because someone in their family died, or maybe their pet died. But everybody has to die someday, usually because they get very old or very sick and their body just stops working. The person or pet that died has an energy that becomes a Spirit but their family is still sad because they will miss them. So you listen to what they say and you tell them you are sorry that they are sad and maybe hold their hand or give them a hug. Then you can be very quiet and help them by feeling love in your heart and imagine sending your love to their heart. We do this because sometimes a person's feelings are deep inside and it is hard for them to talk about it. Sometimes if you are sad, you might just want to be alone and think about things all by yourself and that is okay too. If you are sad then a good thing to do is close your eyes and imagine that you are under water and all your hurt or sadness is in a bubble and you think of your bubble floating up toward the top of the water, and when it gets there the bubble breaks open and all your sadness just disappears with the bubble. Or you could try and remember when you felt happy some other time and keep thinking about that. When I feel as though I want to be alone with my thoughts then I go and float amongst the stars and just watch them twinkle. It makes me feel very calm and quiet and then I feel better. If you feel sad, what do you do to feel better?

But if someone is just feeling a bit grumpy then the Star Travellers play a rhyming game and try to think of as many words that can rhyme with how we feel (I'm grumpy, lumpy, bumpy) and then we start to laugh and forget about why we felt grumpy. Or sometimes we just look in a mirror and tell ourselves, "I love myself, I love my family, I love my friends, I love my pets, I love my house, I love my hair, I love my freckles, I love my baby toe" and before long we are all laughing and feeling good about ourselves and accepting one another just as we are. You should try it the next time you want to change how you are feeling or maybe you can make up another way to the play the game…just use your imagination!

Another great way to feel happy is doing what you love to do. If you love dancing then you should make up some dance moves and just move your body any way that you like because it makes you feel good. If you love singing then you should sing your favourite song or try to make up a new song that no one has heard before. If you can play an instrument and make your own music that would also be fun. You can always ask your friends to play a game you already know or you can all make up a new game and before long you will be enjoying yourselves. If you like to play sports then that works especially well because getting fresh air and exercise can also make you feel good. Drawing pictures is perfect because it's fun and you can draw how you are feeling. You might use bright colours if you are happy or dark colours if you are sad. Once you draw how you feel it might make you feel better. Or you could draw a picture of me! What do you think I look like? Am I big and tall or short and small? Do I have a body shaped like yours or do I look like a cloud or a star? Am I a bright colour or am I invisible? I have already told you I am energy so what do you think that looks like? Use your imagination! The most important thing to remember is feelings are always changing and it is okay to feel angry or sad or afraid sometimes. Everyone does! But it is good to try and feel better too!

If you feel afraid sometimes it is good to think about why you are feeling afraid. It is just a feeling so it can't hurt you and you can try and feel a different way. But first you must try and understand why you feel afraid. If you think a mean dog might bite you, then being afraid helps you to think about what to do and it would be smart to move away from the dog. No one likes to get hurt. But sometimes we are afraid of things for no reason. If you are afraid of the dark and the room isn't any different when the light is on, maybe you could say to yourself, "this is just a silly feeling because I know there is nothing different in the dark". You could use your imagination and believe with all your heart that you are very brave and then talk to the Star Travellers and ask them for help. You could leave the light on at first and keep imagining that you don't really need it and then it will come true. No matter what you might feel you are afraid of, you just have to think if it is real or not. If it is real, then do what you need to do to stay safe, and if it is not real then imagine not being afraid and try doing it again.

You can also do this when you are afraid because of a bad dream. Dreams are just your imagination so they can't hurt you but if you think of something scary like a monster, just say, "Go away monster, I don't want to dream about you. I want to dream about a little puppy or a butterfly or a magic dragon." If you wake up after a bad dream you just say, "No bad dreams" and think of only the nice things you want to dream about. You can think of anything and that way you can decide what you would like the best. But, BEFORE you go to sleep at night you can talk to the Star Travellers and say, "I would like to have fun in my dream tonight" and then tell them what you want to see or do. It is just like using your imagination while you sleep. Isn't that amazing! You could have a dream about doing something fun and going somewhere special. What would you like to dream about? Where will you go? What will you do?

DONT
WALK
WALK
STOP

One of my favourite games is called ***"What if…?"*** and this is a game about choices. So you might decide you want a glass of milk and you think, "What if I try to pour the milk and it spills because it is too heavy for me to lift?" Then you think of another choice and say to yourself, "What if I get my mom to help me and then I can have a glass of milk?" So you make the right choice and ask your mom for help. If you are a little older you might want to go outside but you know you are not supposed to cross the street, so you decide to go outside but you make a choice not to cross the street so that you will be safe. Anytime you think of doing something and there is more than one way to do it, you should ask yourself, "Which choice feels better?"

Sometimes you can ***think*** about choices and sometimes you get a ***feeling*** that you should not do something. This feeling is called ***intuition*** and it is a good feeling to follow. It might be a Star Traveller trying to let you know that they are worried about you and the choice you are about to make. There will be many choices you have to make in your life and sometimes it is your friends who will try and make you do something that maybe you shouldn't, and sometimes it is even adults or strangers who will tell you something that perhaps you shouldn't do. You can always talk to your mom or dad and ask them what they think because they will always try to do what is right for you. You should always try to make the choice that feels right to you, or keeps you safe. Another good choice you can make for yourself is to stay healthy. If you eat healthy food, drinks lots of water, get fresh air and exercise and try to get lots of sleep, then you have made good choices for yourself.

We can also make good choices for the earth. Everything in the world and out in space is a part of ***All That Is***. That includes the earth, sun, stars and moon and every single thing on them and around them; all the plants, animals, insects, birds, fish, people, air and water. All of these things are part of nature and they all help each other to live and this is called ***balance***.

Did you know that the earth turns toward the sun and it is daytime and then keeps turning and it is nighttime? The sun helps everything grow and keeps you warm. Did you know that the moon makes the oceans go higher and lower? This is called tides and the moon is so very strong it can move a whole ocean around the world! The ocean tides help fish and other creatures to stay healthy, and that gives us food to eat. Animals breathe out the air that plants need to live and they provide us with food to eat. Did you know that the trees and plants help to make oxygen which is the air you breathe in so that you can live and grow? The trees and plants also give us food to eat and medicine so that we feel better and stay healthy. Rain helps to fill the rivers and lakes with water so that every living thing has water to drink and even the snow on the mountains melts to give us water. Every living thing needs food to eat, air to breathe, water to drink and shelter so that they can stay warm and protected. You must always be thankful for the plants and animals that provide the food you eat and you should be grateful to have enough water to drink. That is why you must treat Earth like your best friend because if you take care of it then it will take care of you.

All the Star Travellers like to visit Earth and play a game called ***"In a perfect world!"*** In a perfect world you can imagine that you would breathe fresh air and drink clean water. You would enjoy the warm sunshine and have enough food to eat. You would help the animals, birds, fish, insects and plants. You would help to keep the water and the earth clean. You would help other people and you would be happy to see people enjoying the world and taking good care of it. What else would you do in a perfect world? Maybe you can recycle and never throw your garbage on the ground. You can also save energy. You can do that by turning off lights when you leave a room or turning off the tap so you don't waste water. These are all ways that you can play the game called, ***"in a perfect world"***, and it is a good way to help.

You can use all your senses when you are out in nature. Your senses are seeing, hearing, smelling, touching and tasting. You can see the colours of a rainbow or the different colours and shapes of flowers and birds and insects. Birds are fun to watch because when they fly sometimes they work hard to flap their wings and sometimes they just float on the wind. Did you know that people learned how to make airplanes by watching how birds can fly? Have you watched bees when they are going from flower to flower to get pollen? Did you know that flowers need the bees because they help the flowers to make fruit for you to eat? The bees need the pollen from the flowers to make honey. Fruit or honey taste delicious! Have you ever watched a spider make a web? It takes a long time and they can make beautiful designs in their webs. Have you ever watched ants? They are so tiny but they can carry ten to fifty times their body weight! That would be like you trying to carry ten friends, your size, all at once! When something is in an ant's way they just use their imagination and figure out how to get over it or around it. Listen for all the sounds in nature. Can you hear the birds singing, the bees buzzing, the frogs croaking, and the wind blowing or waves splash against the rocks? You can smell the fresh air or the flowers or trees. You can feel nature when you take off your shoes and feel the grass tickle your toes! Or how warm the sand is when you walk along the beach and how cool the water is on your skin. When you touch rocks they can feel hot from the sun or feel cool in the shade and sometimes they are rough or smooth. Did you know rocks can tell a story? When scientists look at rocks they can tell what happened on earth millions of years ago and if it was icy or very hot and sometimes they even find bugs and plants stuck in the rock! Don't forget to look up when you are outside! The clouds are beautiful and even when it is cloudy the sun is still in the sky but it is hidden. Have you seen the stars at night? Did you know the stars are always in the sky but the sun is so bright in the day time that you can't see the stars? Nature is so much fun!

Everything in nature is ***energy.*** The sun, the wind, the water and all the plants and animals all have energy. Have you ever seen lightning? That is LOTS of energy! Spirits are energy just like me. You are energy too, but you have a body and that is how you can run and jump and play. You are able to move and to think and do anything. The last game we shall play is called, ***"I can do anything!"*** You can try to do many different things in your life to see what you enjoy. Maybe you would like to sing and dance or be an actor and then be on TV or in a movie. Perhaps you would like to play sports like soccer, skiing, tennis, baseball or basketball. What other sports could you play? Would you like to be an artist and paint beautiful pictures? You could be an author and write stories. What would you write about? Maybe you could be a scientist and discover a new kind of medicine. What else might a scientist discover? You could use your imagination and invent something that people really need. What do you think it might be? Maybe you would like to be an astronaut and fly up into space. Maybe you will see me there and we can talk to each other just by thinking! You can do anything! What do you think you could be? What would you like to try? Do not worry if you try and make a mistake or can't do it because that is how you learn. Each time you try something, you become better at doing it. When you were a little baby you didn't know how to walk or talk but you kept trying and then you learned how. You are very smart! Things are always changing and that is okay too, because that is how you learn. If you do something one day and it works and then it doesn't work the next day, you learn how to make changes. You do things a different way and that makes it interesting. Do not be sad or mad when things change or don't always work the way you want them to because sometimes you just have to try harder or use your imagination and think of a new way to do it. If you always try your best, then that is what is important and you can feel good about yourself!

"Sending Love and Light"

So, now we have talked about loving yourself and being kind to others. You have learned about your feelings and how to be happy and how to make good choices. We have taught you about using your imagination to do anything you want and that the Star Travellers are here to help you even in your dreams. We have told you how to take care of the earth and about some of the plants and animals and how to have fun outdoors in nature. You have learned about the sun and the moon and the stars and Space. You have also learned about Star Travellers and that we are Spirits who travel amongst the stars and you have learned about All That Is.

We have asked you to keep your heart wide open. If you keep your heart wide open then you will have love for everyone and everything in the whole world. If you can keep your mind wide open too then you will always be willing to listen to new ideas and try new things. Always use your imagination and really believe you can do anything and you can make it happen. We hope you can remember all these things and that you will play the games we have taught you because they will help you to remember. Teach your friends these games and maybe one day you will all teach these games to your children!

We have told you about many wonderful things so that you know some of our secrets and so that you can make changes in the world right now and when you grow up. We have done this because we know you will be able to do all you can imagine and that you will try very hard to make things better for other people and for the world. The Star Travellers are always close by so you are never alone and we will always try to help you and keep you safe. All the Star Travellers are your friends and we will always listen when you speak to us. Please don't forget about us or what we have tried to teach you!

We send you our love and light.

ABOUT THE AUTHOR

Wendy Pierce worked for over 32 years in elementary schools and also taught Sunday school for children aged 3-5 years. She has her Master of Divinity degree and recently obtained her Doctorate degree in Philosopher of Metaphysics.

Dr. Pierce is now retired and living on Vancouver Island, B.C. She has two children, a granddaughter and a great-granddaughter.

ACKNOWLEDGEMENTS

I would like to express my love and heartfelt gratitude to my family and friends for their support and encouragement, and especially, to Paul Biscop, Ph.D., for his help with proofreading and editing. My eternal gratitude to Natalie Fischer, for bringing my story to life with her beautiful illustrations. See more of her work at www.nataliefischer.ca